SERGER SHORTCUTS

TIPS, TRICKS & TECHNIQUES

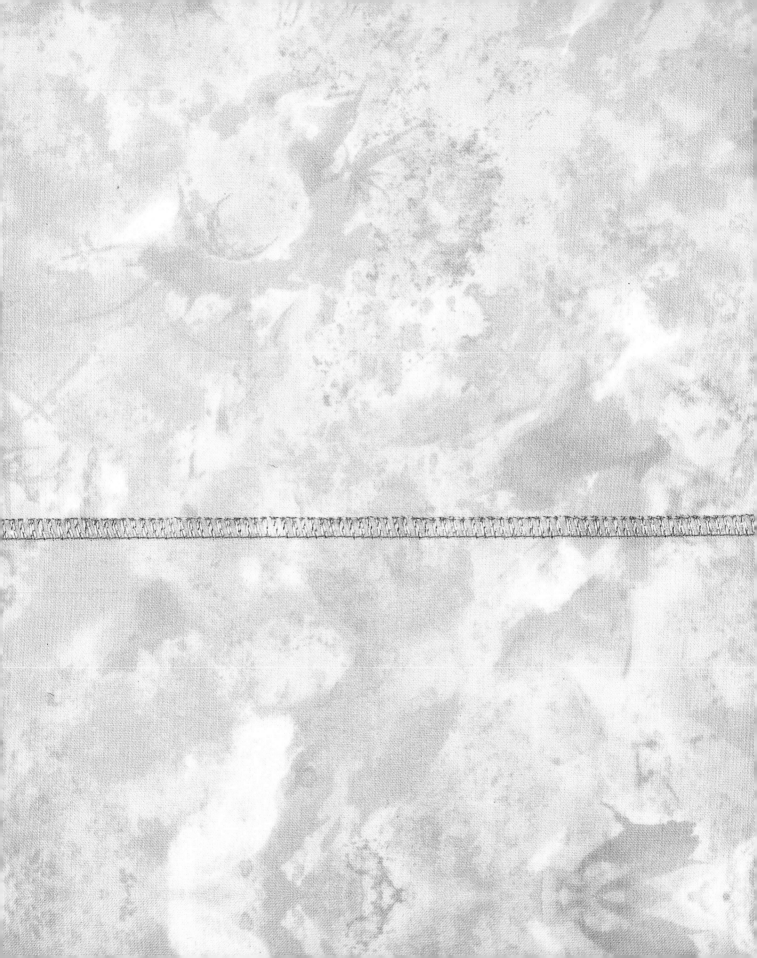

SERGER SHORTCUTS
TIPS, TRICKS & TECHNIQUES

JoAnn Pugh-Gannon and Pamela J. Hastings

Sterling Publishing Co., Inc.

New York

A Sterling/Sewing Information Resources Book

Sewing Information Resources

Owner: JoAnn Pugh-Gannon
Photography: Kaz Ayukawa, K Graphics
Book Design and Electronic Page Layout: Ernie Shelton, Shelton Design Studios
Illustrations: Ernie Shelton
Copy Editor: Barbara Patterson
Index: Mary Helen Schiltz

Sewing Information Resources is a registered trademark of GANZ Inc.

Library of Congress Cataloging-in-Publication Data

JoAnn Pugh-Gannon and Hastings, Pamela J.
    The complete sewing machine handbook / by JoAnn Pugh-Gannon
    and Hastings, Pamela J.
        p.   cm.
    "A Sterling/Sewing Information Resources book."
    Includes bibliographical references and index.
    ISBN 0-8069-0848-3
    1. Machine sewing. 2. Sewing machines. I. Title.
TT713.K86   1997
646.2'044--dc21   97-41176
                                                                    CIP

A Sterling/Sewing Information Resources Book

1   3   5   7   9   10   8   6   4   2

First paperback edition published in 1999 by
Sterling Publishing Company, Inc.
387 Park Avenue South, New York, N.Y. 10016
© 1998 by JoAnn Pugh-Gannon & Pamela J. Hastings
Distributed in Canada by Sterling Publishing
℅ Canadian Manda Group, One Atlantic Avenue, Suite 105
Toronto, Ontario, Canada M6K 3E7
Distributed in Great Britain and Europe by Cassell PLC
Wellington House, 125 Strand, London WC2R 0BB, England
Distributed in Australia by Capricorn Link (Australia) Pty Ltd.
P.O. Box 6651, Baulkham Hills, Business Centre, NSW 2153, Australia
Printed in China
All rights reserved

Sterling ISBN 0-8069-0838-6 Trade
0-8069-2455-1 Paper

About the Authors

JoAnn Pugh-Gannon

JoAnn has been involved in the home sewing industry for many years. Her first position as an educational representative with Simplicity Pattern Company led to a long career with Swiss Bernina, later known as Bernina of America, the United States importer of Swiss-made Bernina sewing machines and related products. As Vice-President of Marketing Software for Bernina, she was responsible for all dealer and consumer education.

In 1994, she started Sewing Information Resources, a packager and publisher of sewing and craft books.

Pamela J. Hastings

Pam began her sewing career working for several companies in the home sewing industry. She has made numerous guest appearances on national and local television programs, hosted a sewing program on the Home and Garden Network as a spokesperson for the Singer Sewing Company as well as appeared in, wrote, and coordinated the Butterick "Sew by Video" series. She currently serves as spokesperson for several companies within the sewing industry.

She also is the author of the Sterling/ Sewing Information Resources book, *Creative Sewing Projects with Computerized Machines.*

After having worked together on numerous free-lance projects over the past four years, JoAnn and Pam pooled their vast sewing knowledge and collaborated on *Serger Shortcuts: Tips, Tricks & Techniques.*

SERGER SHORTCUTS
TIPS, TRICKS & TECHNIQUES

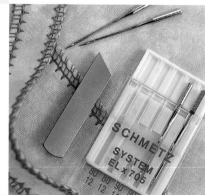

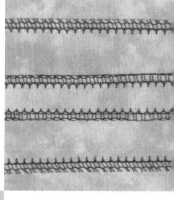
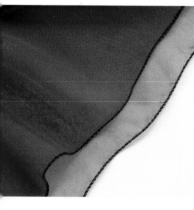

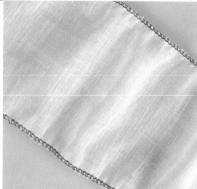

Introduction

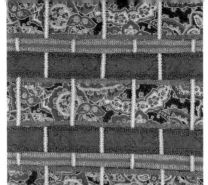

To many people, using the words *serger* and *shortcuts* in the same sentence is redundant. A serger, or overlock machine, in and of itself, makes sewing faster and easier. However, like anything in life, the machine provides those benefits in relation to how much the operator knows. In other words, the more you know how to use your serger, the more shortcuts you can find and take.

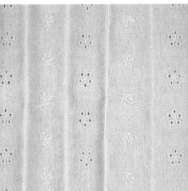

There are many serger brands on the market today. Manufacturers offer similar features, as well as different and unique stitch combinations. It's up to you, as an educated shopper, to determine which machine is most appropriate for your sewing needs. Whatever type of machine you own—2-, 3-, 4-, 5-thread, or any combination thereof—the shortcuts illustrated here will help you. Try some or try them all, but we hope you will find tips or tricks that make your serging easier. And, in the process of learning more about your machine, you also will discover your own shortcuts.

Chapter 1

Among the most important elements of your serger or

overlock machine are the needles, the knives, and the

tension dials (controls). A quality needle—appropriately

sized for the fabric—is essential. Just a small nick

or burr on the needle can cause your stitch to form

Needles, Knives, and Tension

improperly. Two sharp knives allow clean cuts in the

fabric. Maintaining your knife blades is vital. And last

but not least, understanding the function and use of

the tension dials, as well as keeping the tension disks

clean, makes for happy serging.

Needles

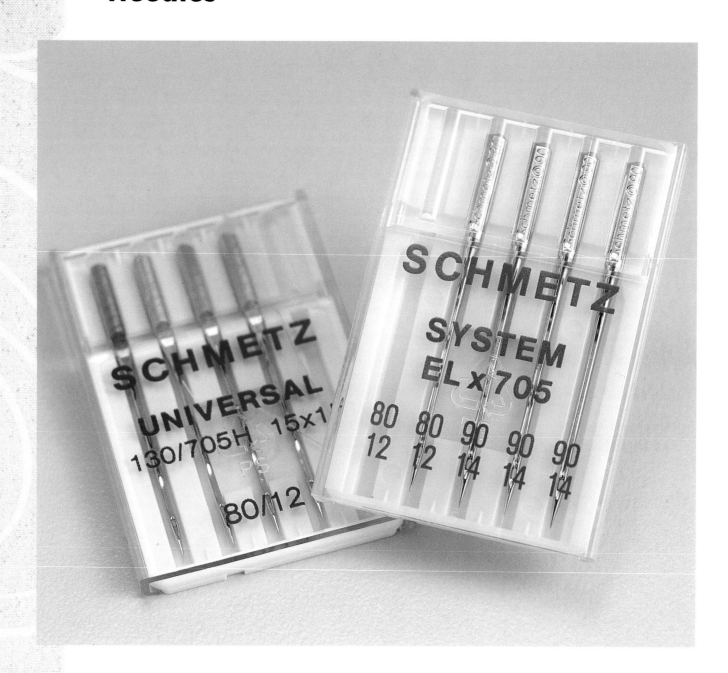

Needle Size

Selecting the correct needle for every project is important. Most sergers can handle almost any size needle indicated for the fabric that you are serging. Be sure to check your serger instruction manual for the needle sizes appropriate to your machine.

Burrs and Other Problems

Generally, needles between sizes #70/10 and #90/14 work on most machines. By selecting a larger size, the chance of the needle hitting the looper becomes greater, causing damage to your machine. If you are using a heavier thread, consider selecting a topstitching needle within the size range appropriate to your machine.

Topstitching needles have larger eyes to accommodate the heavier threads. By using a topstitching needle for heavier threads, you are solving two problems at once—protecting your machine from damage caused by too big of a needle and accommodating the heavy thread with a larger needle eye.

Skipped stitches happen when serging, just as they do when sewing with your conventional sewing machine. And generally, the reason for this problem is the same—a bent or burred needle. The solution to the problem is quick and easy just change the needle!

You can easily tell if there is a burr on the needle point by gently passing your finger down the shank to the tip of the needle. You will be able to feel the slightly rough edge or blunt point.

Burrs and Other Problems *continued*

Check for a bent needle by laying the needle, flat side of the shank down, on a tabletop and pressing down with your finger on the shank. By looking at the needle from the side, you can tell if the needle is parallel to the table or not. A bent needle needs replacing.

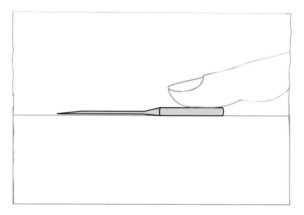

If you are experiencing thread breakage while you are serging, again the needle may be the cause. The thread may be catching on a rough spot in the needle eye, causing the thread to break. Your best bet is to change the needle first to see if that solves your stitching problems. Needles are not as perfect as we might think they are. Often a bad needle is the reason for your problems.

When serging, be careful not to pull the fabric through the machine, since this may cause the needle to break or bend. A broken needle can cause damage to one of the loopers, nick the needle plate, or create a burr on the serger presser foot. Be careful when serging not to pull the fabric through the machine causing the needle to break or bend.

Often these burrs are visible to the eye, though sometimes they can't be detected visually. Run your finger along the edge of all of the loopers to feel for burrs. Check the tips for burred points. Be careful because the looper tips are very sharp!

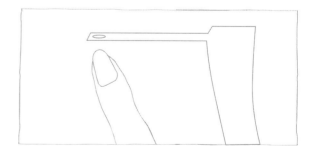

Check the needle plate near the stitch fingers for small "catches" that can break threads. Or look around the needle hole with a magnifying glass to see if there are any notches or nicks that will hook the threads.

The presser foot can develop burrs from constant use. Feel the bottom for any rough spots developed from hours and hours of serging. Also check around the needle area, as a broken needle may have accidentally hit the foot.

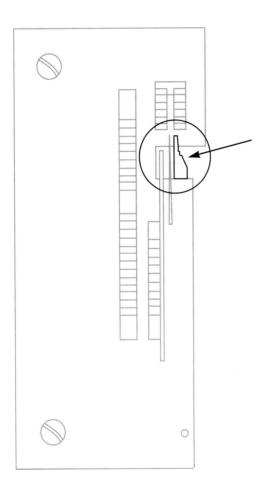

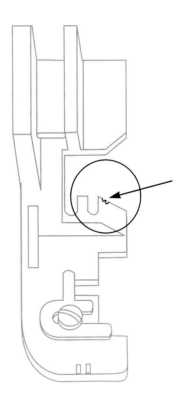

Burrs and Other Problems *continued*

A small piece of Crocus Cloth from the hardware store or your sewing notions catalog can help you rectify your "burr problem." Try these solutions with caution, but remember a call to your serger repair person should be made for any major damage done to your machine.

The Crocus Cloth can be cut into narrow strips and used to remove burrs from the needle hole or on the stitch finger on the needle plate. Gentle rubbing is all that's is necessary to remove most nicks or burrs.

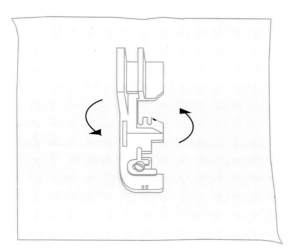

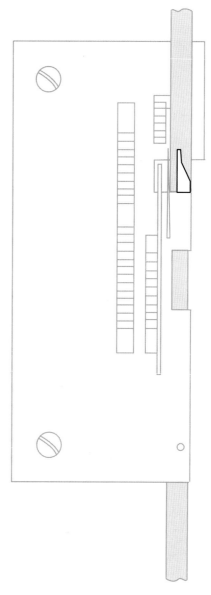

Lay the Crocus Cloth flat on the tabletop and place the bottom of the presser foot down on the surface. Rub in a circular motion to remove any rough spots on the bottom of the foot.

Knives

There are two knives used on the serger that move in a scissors-like motion, cutting the fabric while you are stitching. The location of these knives (upper and lower) may not necessarily be in the same place on all brands of machines, but their importance is the same. One blade remains in a fixed position while the other moves, duplicating the scissors-like action.

Damaged Knives

Thread breakage, fabric jamming, or fabric snagging may be a few of the symptoms of a dull or damaged knife(s). Knife blades dull after much use and need to be replaced. Generally, your machine will come with a replacement upper or lower blade. Check your instruction manual for information on how to remove and replace the damaged or worn blade.

Accidentally serging over pins can cause a knife to be damaged, so care should be taken when serging in tight or difficult areas. Be sure to remove the pins before reaching the blades.

If you find that there is damage to the blade you cannot replace, call your sewing machine dealer for service. This knife blade needs to be installed by your dealer and properly aligned with the blade you replaced.

Care and Maintenance

Prolong the life of your serger knives by keeping them clean and oiling them when necessary.

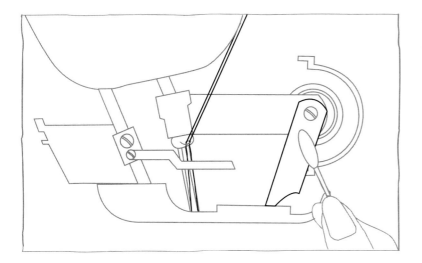

Clean the blades with a Q-Tip™ dipped in alcohol. This will remove any lint buildup or old oil left on the blades.

Apply a thin film of oil on the inside of the blades (metal against metal) after they have been cleaned. Make sure the blades are back in their proper position, then run the machine to distribute the oil evenly. With a little care, your serger knives will last you through many, many projects.

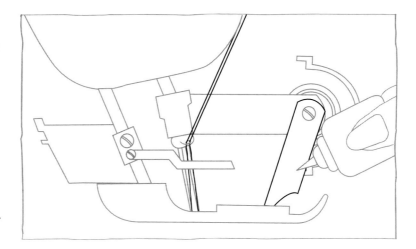

Tension

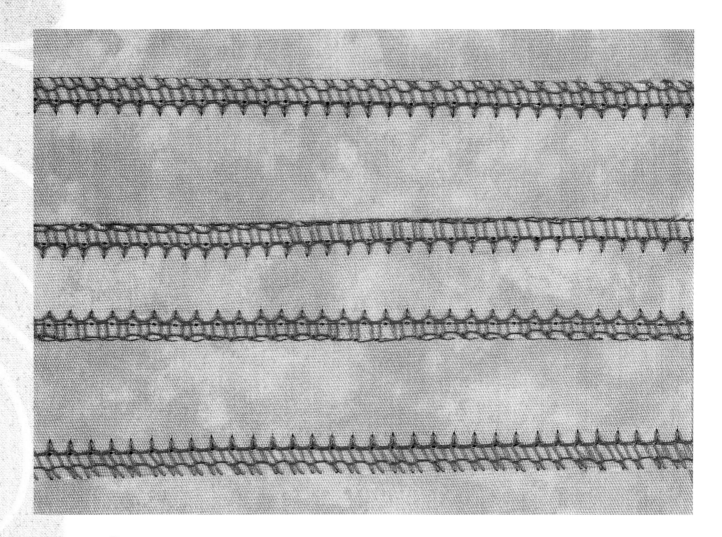

Often the first complaint or statement made by a sewer about her serger, or overlock machine, is that the "tension is off" or "I just can't seem to get the tension right." Before doing anything else, make sure the tension disks on your machine are clean. Simply run a length of knotted thread or a piece of folded muslin between the tension disks, removing any lint or oil buildup. Rethread your machine, making sure the thread is "locked" into the tension disks correctly and all threading paths are used for that stitch formation.

Many times, changing the needle or the cutting width will correct what is perceived as a tension problem without turning the dials. Even adjusting the differential feed, if your machine has this feature, can affect the stitch. Check these three points first, before starting to turn your tension dials.

Puckers

Poor stitches are often characterized as puckered stitches. Check to make sure your stitch is wide enough to cover the edge and lie flat. A too-narrow stitch may look like puckers, but it really doesn't require a tension adjustment.

After each tension adjustment, serge off a stitch sample. Mark each sample with the adjustment made for reference and comparison. To eliminate puckers, first loosen the needle tension; continue loosening until the stitch lies flat. If loosening the needle tension isn't enough, slightly adjust the looper tensions.

Puckers *continued*

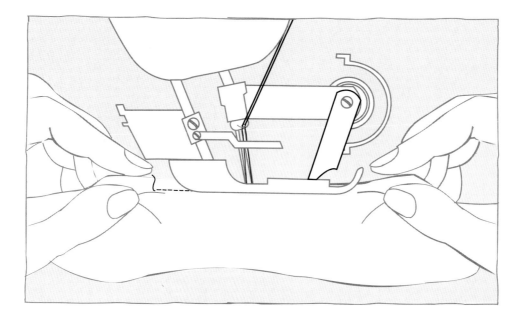

Another solution to prevent puckers is what is referred to as "taut-serging." By holding the fabric firmly from behind and in front of the presser foot, the fabric will remain flat. Be very careful not to pull the fabric while you are stitching. This technique also is often used when sewing on fine or silky fabrics on the sewing machine. If neither of these solutions work, try a shorter stitch length; use a finer needle or finer thread; stabilize the seam with Seams Great® (see Chapter Three, "Beautiful Rolled Hems on Sheers") or another form of stabilization; or increase the presser foot pressure. You may have to use a combination of the above solutions to solve your puckering problem.

Tension Adjustments and the Rolled Hem

Tension adjustments are necessary for forming a perfect rolled-hem stitch. Depending on your machine, select the rolled-hem setting that is preprogrammed for you (fine-tuning may stilled be needed on your fabric), or adjust the machine as follows. Also choose the appropriate stitch formation (2-thread or 3-thread) and thread for the weight of fabric being rolled. A 2-thread rolled hem is usually preferred for very fine fabrics, such as batiste, fine silk, or chiffon.

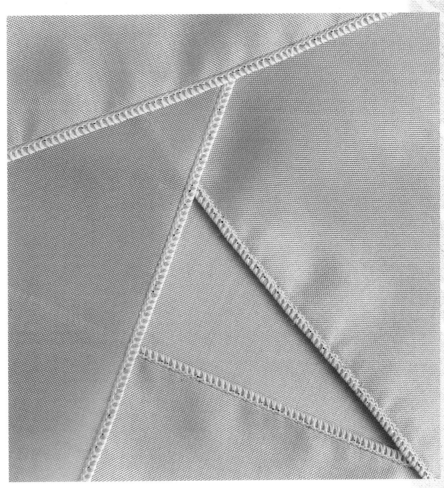

Change the throat plate to a rolled-hem plate or move the wide stitch finger out of the way. Remove the left needle if necessary. Tighten the lower looper to the highest tension. You may need to slightly loosen the upper looper and tighten the needle. Test your rolled hem. Fine-tune as needed. If necessary, "taut-serge" to eliminate any puckering.

If your rolled hem still needs adjustment, remember—not every fabric will roll successfully. But you still can try the following: Check your cutting width to see how much or how little fabric is being trimmed away. Try a Woolly Nylon® thread in the lower looper and adjust the tension accordingly. Shorten the stitch length. Stabilize the edge if the fabric is very fine or if the stitching is pulling away from the edge.

Chapter 2

From functional to decorative, a wide range of

threads are available for use on a serger. All-purpose

threads in a multitude of colors are used for

constructing projects and for some decorative

techniques, such as pintucks and flatlock ribbon

weaving. Decorative threads take serging one step

further and turn a basic 3-thread overlock stitch into

a "braid-like" finishing touch. Experiment with a

variety of threads and fabrics to discover your own

favorite techniques.

Functional Threads

Functional threads are the ones you use when actually constructing a garment or home decorating project. These threads may be purchased on parallel- or cross-wound spools, tubes, or cones, but in any case, it is important to use quality thread. Quality thread is smooth and will have few fibers sticking out; it also will perform well in your serger. Inferior thread (bargain thread) often has thick and thin spots and sometimes knots. This thread will be difficult to use, as the weak spots may cause breakage, and the thick and thin spots may cause tension problems. The quality of the thread you use for functional serging is far more important than whether it is on a spool or a cone.

The type of thread you will use for most of your serging is available on cones or spools. Invest in cones in neutral colors or staple colors like black and white. Use spools when you are making a garment and you would like all the loops to match the fabric, but you do not need the quantity of thread found on a cone. When using traditional spools, be sure to top parallel-wound spools with a thread cap to prevent the thread from getting caught on any notches in the top of the spool.

When using all-purpose thread, do not be afraid to blend colors. If you are using your serger to construct a seam, the needle thread should match your fabric. You may choose the looper threads to blend with your fabric.

Decorative Threads

Decorative threads can be used to create beautiful edge finishes, such as rolled hems, or unique details on a project, such as flatlocking. There is a wide assortment of decorative threads to choose from; you can create virtually any effect you desire, depending on the thread you select. Yarns give a more classic feel, metallics a holiday appearance, and Woolly Nylon® the perfect edging. Following is a selection of decorative threads that are worth experimenting with.

Fine Rayon—Traditionally used for embroidery, rayon thread works well on 2-thread rolled hems on sheer or lightweight fabric. Rayon is also nice to use when stitching small pintucks and for heirloom techniques. Rayon is available on parallel- or cross-wound spools or tubes. If you are using tubes, you will find that the thread may slip off the tube and get caught on the serger. If this happens, simply place the tube in a juice glass on the sewing surface behind your serger, and the thread will feed smoothly.

Fine Metallic—These threads include metallic embroidery threads and very shiny threads called Tinsel or Sliver. These threads are great for decorative techniques and may be combined with other threads for an interesting effect.

Decorative Threads *continued*

Textured Nylon—Commonly known as Woolly Nylon®, this thread is available on cones and in an endless assortment of colors and variegated tones. This thread looks like all-purpose thread on the cone, but when it is unwound, it fluffs up. This fluffing will fill in space between stitches, covering the fabric underneath. It is perfect for edge-finishing, rolled hems, and constructing swimwear and leotards.

Heavyweight Rayon—Heavy rayon thread is available on cones as Designer 6 or Pearl Crown and on spools as Decor 6. Rayon is very shiny and is available in brilliant colors. It definitely makes a statement when used for decorative techniques. This thread may be used in the upper looper for flatlocking or in upper and lower loopers when edge-finishing. Try making reversible place mats, and use coordinating colors in each looper. Parallel-wound spools tend to spill off the spool and sometimes get tangled; for best results, place spools on the sewing surface behind your serger or use a thread net for better thread control.

Decorative Threads *continued*

Heavyweight Metallic Threads—Available on cones, tubes, or spools, Candlelight and Glamour are soft, metallic, yarn-like threads that are used for decorative techniques.

Although they are used for the same techniques as heavy rayon threads, the look is quite different. These threads are much more festive and glamorous—the perfect touch on holiday linens and garments.

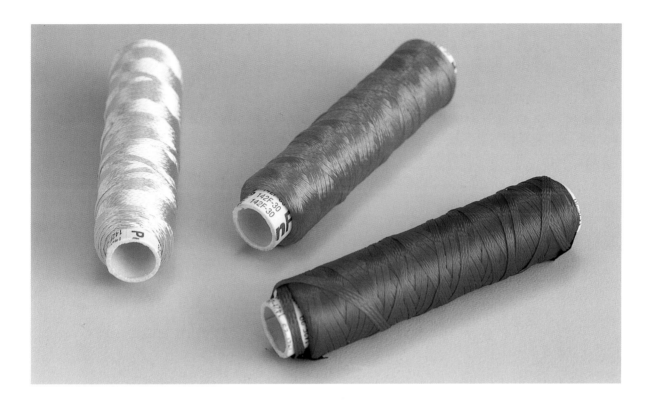

Ribbon Floss—For a different look on decorative techniques, try using ribbon floss. Used for hand embroidery, ribbon floss is available on tubes and in skeins. When using tubes, place in a juice glass or on a horizontal thread holder. When using skeins, it will be necessary to hand-wind the ribbon floss around a cone to feed it into the serger.

Yarns—Yarn specifically packaged for serger use, called Success, is available on cross-wound cones in a wide range of colors. Yarn has more of a textured matte finish and adds a classic look for decorative techniques on wool or corduroy. Any 3-ply baby- or sport-weight yarn

may be used. As with ribbon floss, it will be necessary to wind any yarn not packaged for sergers onto a cone before using.

Chapter 3

The serger can elevate your garment sewing to a

higher level. Your finished pieces will have the

appearance of ready-to-wear and your sewing time

will be cut in half. Seaming, applying zippers, or

even repairing stretched-out elastic bands can be

Garment Construction

accomplished on your serger quickly and easily.

Experiment with the tips, tricks, and techniques

given here on your next serger project.

Easy Flat-Fell Seams

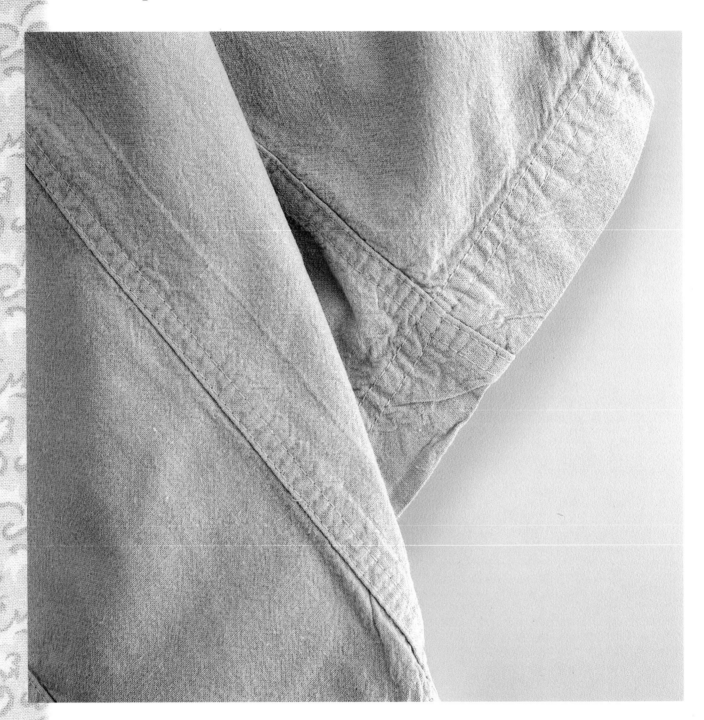

A flat-fell seam is the perfect, sporty, clean finish for sturdy fabrics such as denim, twill, or wool. Completed in two steps, this serger seam is easy and attractive.

1 Serge-finish the edges of the fabric pieces. Stitch a standard ⅝″ seam allowance, offsetting one layer of fabric by ¼″. Press both edges of the seam allowance to one side, the wider edge over the narrower edge.

2 Topstitch from the right side with a 6 mm double needle, stitching down the seam allowance. **Note:** If you own a coverstitch machine with a hem guide, this technique can be completed in one step.

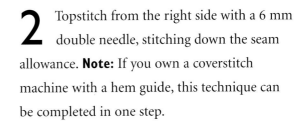

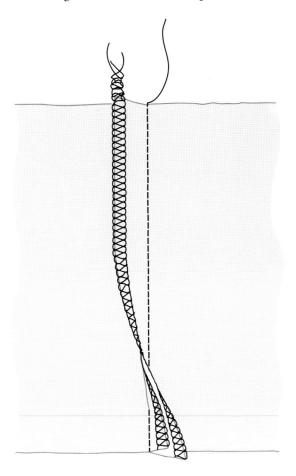

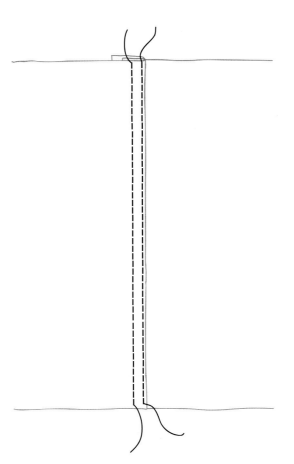

Beautiful Rolled Hems on Sheers

Sheer fabrics can be tricky to sew without even considering a rolled edge. These slippery or wiry fabrics pose unique problems when rolled, such as "pokies"—little thread ends that poke through the rolled edge—develope or the edge pulls away from the garment. Follow these instructions for beautiful rolled edges on sheers.

1 First, test on scraps of fabric to get the results you desire. Use a fine needle, such as a #60/8 or #70/10; select a fine thread, a #50- or #60-weight cotton, a soft Woolly Nylon® or a fine rayon; and adjust the machine for a 2- or 3-thread rolled hem.

2 To guarantee a straight hem, mark the hem by pulling a thread across the fabric. For more stability on the edge when stitching, fold back the hem along the pulled thread and press. **Note:** On some sheer fabrics, it may not be necessary to fold back the edge; just trim the fabric along the pulled thread.

3 To eliminate pokies, cut a piece of Seams Great® (a narrow piece of nylon tricot fabric) or water-soluble stabilizer, and place halfway under the fabric edge. As you serge, guide the fabric just to the left of the knife marking on the serger foot. After serging, use appliqué scissors to trim the excess fabric and Seams Great® from the back close to the stitching.

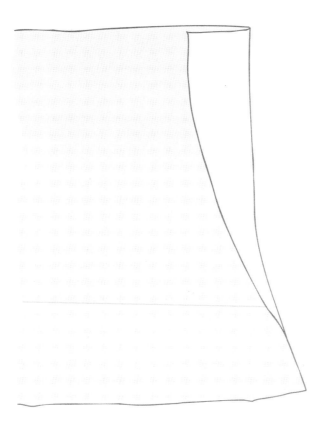

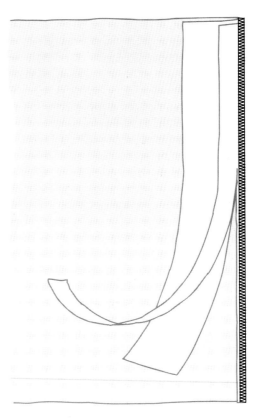

Perfect Corners on Sheers

1 Roll the edge along one side of the piece following the instructions above.

2 Before rolling the second edge, place the sheer fabric between two pieces of water-soluble stabilizer at the corner. Pin in place to avoid slipping. Begin serging a chain before serging onto the fabric. Hold the chain taut and serge onto the stabilizer and fabric at the corner.

3 Remove the stabilizer by trimming or rinsing with water. Trim the thread chain and dab the corner threads with Fray Check®.

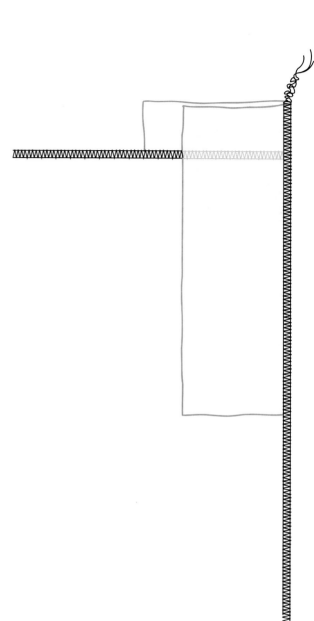

Fishline Ruffles

Nancy Jewell, Husqvarna Viking®

A stand-up ruffle is achieved by adding fishline to a rolled hem edge on any garment.

1 Adjust your machine for a 3-thread rolled hem. You can use a decorative thread in the upper looper if desired. Thread the fishline through the specialty technique guide and into the guide hole on the presser foot. Stitch two to three stitches, catching the fishline in the stitching.

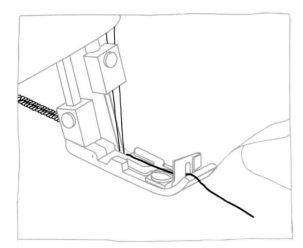

2 Insert a long strip of fabric under the foot and guide the fabric and fishline with your right hand; hold the fishline tail with your left hand to begin stitching.

3 After finishing the rolled edge, gather the opposite edge. Increase the differential feed setting to the machine's highest point and use the longest stitch length. Attach to the flat fabric with a balanced 4-thread stitch.

Coverstitch Topstitching

The coverstitch, found on some serger models, is easily adaptable to topstitching. A straight stitch appears on the top and a flat cover-serge stitch is on the reverse side of the fabric. Either side can be used for topstitching detail.

1 Measure and turn up the hem of the garment. For a traditional coverstitch topstitch, thread each needle (2 or 3) with the desired thread. Remember to use a larger-eyed needle if you are using a heavier thread in the needles. Stitch the hem from the right side. **Note:** Some brands of sergers have hem guides available for guiding the fabric evenly.

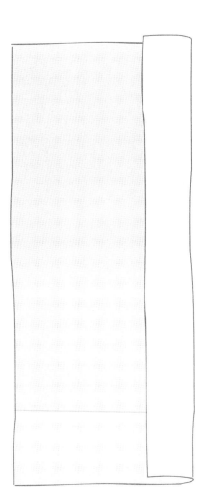

2 For a decorative hem using the cover-serge stitch on the outside, stitch with the right side of the fabric down. Select the decorative thread of choice and thread the looper. Stitch the hem. **Note:** Some fine-tuning of your tensions will be necessary since you are using different weights of thread. Turn the fabric to the right side to see the cover-serge stitch.

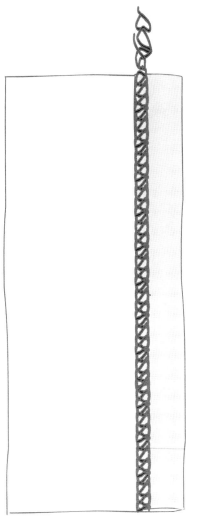

Zippers

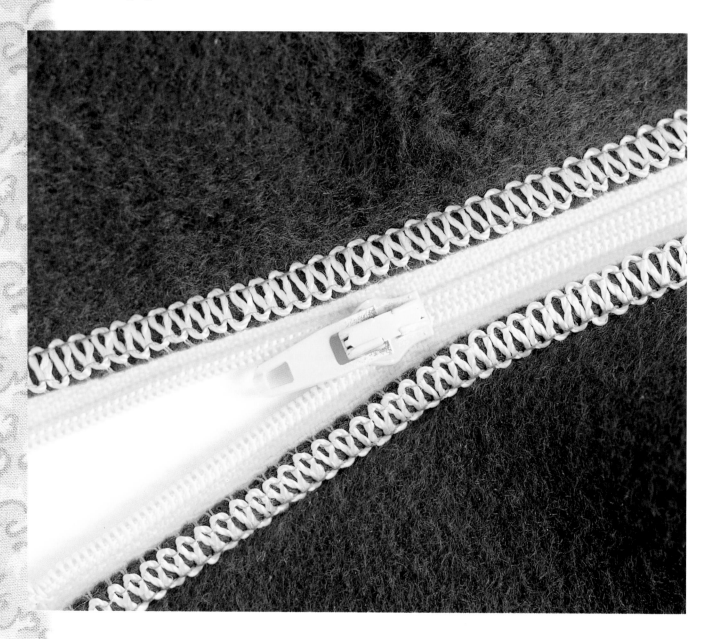

Serged, Lapped, and Topstitched

The serged, lapped, and topstitched zipper application is perfect for tightly woven fabrics or fun fleece. A heavy rayon or other tightly twisted decorative threads can be used in the upper looper to add detail to the garment. This technique works well with either separating or placket zippers.

I Adjust the serger for a wide 3-thread overlock stitch using your thread of choice in the upper looper and a shorter stitch length. For a separating zipper, serge-finish the edges trimming back the seam allowance. For a placket application, cut open the placket and serge-finish the edge trimming back approximately ¼″ from each side while serging. (For the placket application, you may choose to use a narrow, short 3-thread stitch rather than a wide 3-thread stitch.)

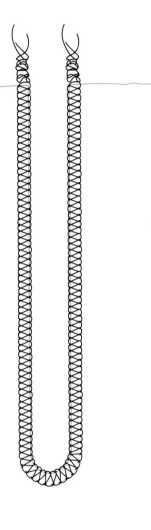

Serged, Lapped, and Topstitched *continued*

2 Lap the serge-finished edges over the zipper tape leaving the zipper teeth exposed. Pin or adhere the fabric in place with a fabric glue stick.

3 Topstitch the fabric in place next to the serger stitch with your sewing machine.

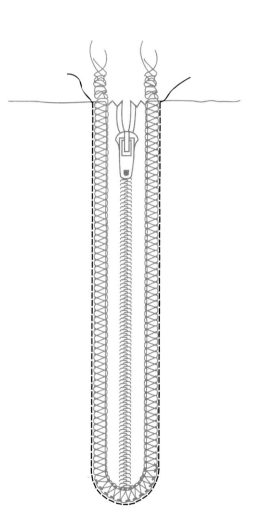

Zipper Application with Fusible Thread

Fusible thread can save steps in your sewing and serging. Use it in the upper looper and press-baste the fabric in place before inserting the zipper. Everything is held in place while you are stitching.

1 Serge-finish the zipper opening using fusible thread in the upper looper. Turn back the edges to the wrong side and fuse in place.

2 Place the zipper in the opening and stitch in place catching the fused edges in the stitching at the same time.

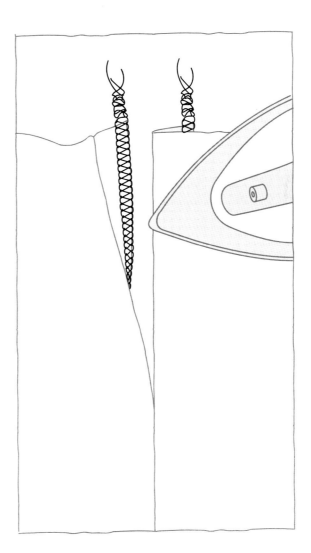

Perfect Jacket or Collar Points

Making sharp, crisp points can be tricky. For a practically foolproof corner application, try this serging method.

1 With right sides together, serge along the long edge or outside edge of the collar. Press the seam flat, then press the seam toward the under collar.

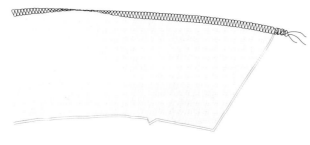

2 Serge each short end of the collar, stitching over the seam allowance that was folded back. Press the seams flat, then turn the collar point to the right side. Use a point turner if necessary. Press again.

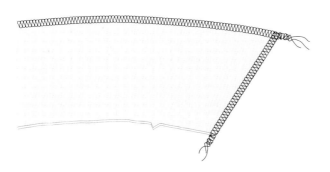

Stabilizing Ribbing

Often the neckline or cuff ribbing on a well-loved T-shirt or turtleneck will become stretched out of shape. With the help of clear elastic, the shape of the ribbing can be recovered easily.

1 Measure the diameter of your wrist or the desired neckline opening. Cut the elastic to this length plus 1″.

2 Find the center of the elastic and the center front of the neckline or cuff. Match marks and pin. Stretch the elastic to meet and overlap ½″ at the opposite side. Pin in place.

3 Using a 4-thread stitch, serge the elastic to the ribbing seam stretching the elastic while serging. The ribbing will be recovered to it's original shape.

Quick-and-Easy Circular Ribbing

Nancy Jewell, Husqvarna Viking

Try this quick-and-easy serger application for sewing ribbing at necklines or cuffs. It's foolproof!

Quick-and-Easy Circular Ribbing *continued*

1 Cut your ribbing twice the desired width plus two seam allowances and two-thirds the desired length of the opening.

2 Fold the ribbing in half with short ends together. Fold in half again with long edges together. There are now four layers crosswise and lengthwise.

3 Serge along the short edge using a balanced 3- or 4-thread stitch formation.

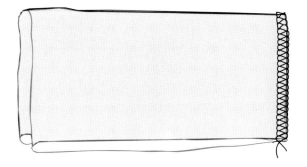

4 Turn one layer back over the seam as if you are folding socks. Your circular ribbing is done!

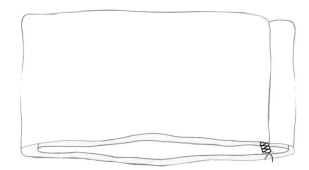

Mock-Piped Binding

For a creative decorative touch, add mock-piped binding to the edge of a garment. A rolled edge is applied to one edge of the bias strip before binding your jacket or vest.

Mock-Piped Binding *continued*

1 Cut your bias strips the length of the area
to be bound. The width is the desired
width of the binding plus ½" plus ¼" for turn.

2 Select a decorative thread for the rolled
edge—metallic, Woolly Nylon®, or rayon
threads work well. Thread the upper looper
with the decorative thread and adjust your
machine for a rolled edge.

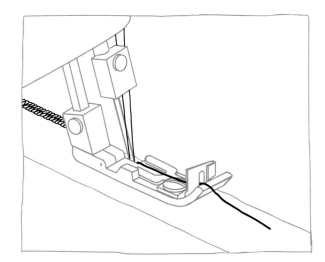

3 Using a cording, beading, or piping foot
(if available for your machine), place a
filler cord in the groove of the foot and roll edge
over the cord along the right side of one long
edge of the bias strip.

4 With the wrong side of the garment to the right side of the bias strip, match raw edges. Serge the binding to the garment.

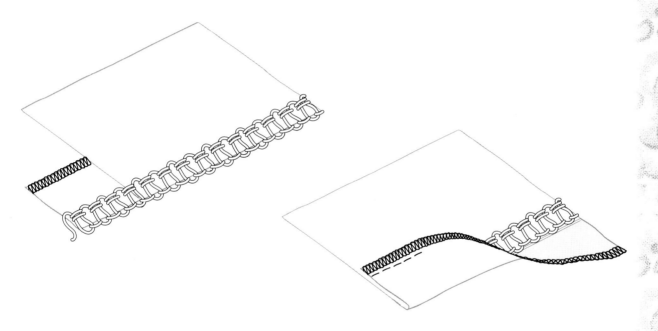

5 Wrap the binding strip to the right side and straight-stitch in place next to the rolled edge.

Pin-Weaving with the Serger

Laura Haynie, Pfaff American Sales Corp.

Design your own fabric by weaving decoratively serged strips of fabric and trim together. Fused to a lightweight interfacing, your weaving can be treated as your fabric.

1 Select a group of three to four coordinating print fabrics. Cut your fabrics into strips, varying the widths for more interest. Thread your serger using a decorative metallic thread, such as Candlelight metallic yarn, in the upper looper. Serge both edges of the fabric strips.

2 Using the taping foot, place soutache braid into the foot and under the front guide; hold in place with the adjusting screw. Serge over the braid to create decorative cord for weaving.

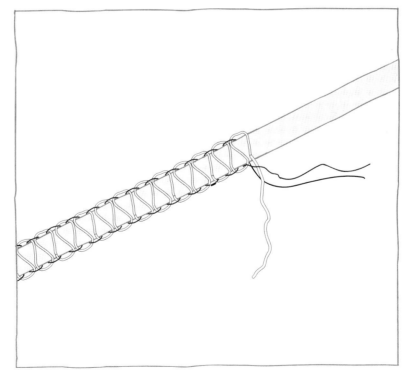

3 Cut a piece of Easy Knit®, or any other lightweight fusible interfacing, to the desired size to be woven and place on a pinable working surface. Arrange the serged strips horizontally across the interfacing, butting the edges. Fuse the ends along the left edge.

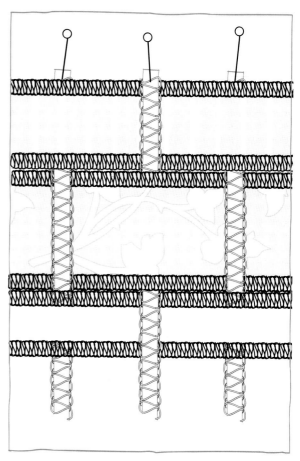

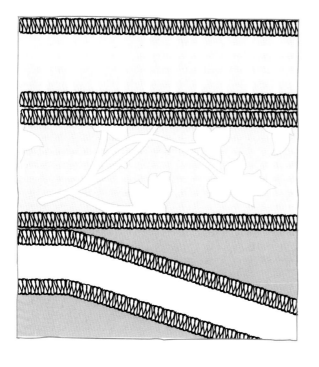

4 Pin the decorative cord across the top at even intervals (1″ – 2″ apart). Weave the cord over and under the fabric strips, creating your fabric. Fuse all the strips and cords to the interfacing and cut out your pattern from the "new" fabric.

Heirloom Pintucks

Laura Haynie, Pfaff American Sales Corp.

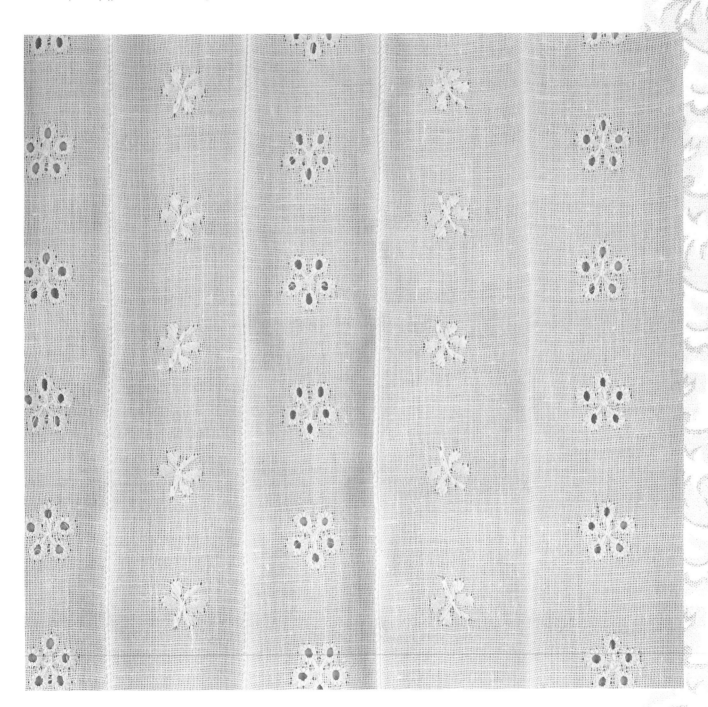

Add beautiful, delicate pintucks to eyelet fabric and sew up a sweet heirloom dress suitable for any little girl or her favorite doll.

1 Thread the serger for a 3-thread rolled hem using a tone-on-tone rayon thread in the upper looper. Adjust your serger accordingly for a 3-thread rolled-hem stitch.

2 Press creases the length of the eyelet fabric to be used, spacing them evenly between the embroideries.

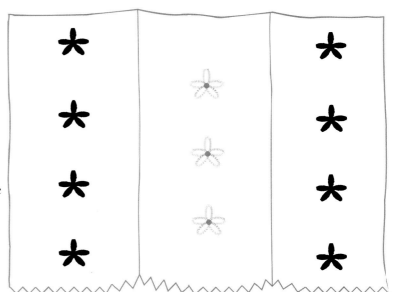

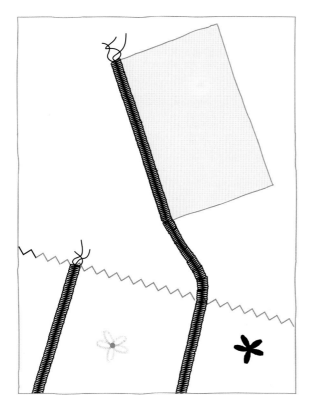

3 Begin serging on a small square of stabilizer to get your rolled hem started and to give you something to hold onto when starting. Using the lace sewing foot, place the pressed edges of the eyelet fabric against the guide and continue serging. The guide on the foot will help keep your rows of pintucks straight and even.

Tips from the Experts

Sara Meyer, Bernina of America

Three-Needle Coverstitch Applications

Using three needles and the lower looper, this unique stitch formation can be used either as a construction stitch or a decorative stitch. Often used along the hem of stretch fabrics, the three-needle coverstitch is very durable for active wear providing both stretch and strength. To add a decorative touch to the garment, use your choice of decorative threads in the lower looper. Stitch on the wrong side, and unlimited creative possibilities open up for you.

A Practical 2-Thread Chainstitch Application

Marlis Bennett, Bernina of America

When hemming garments that will be worn by someone else in the future, such as costumes, choir robes, band uniforms, and so on, use a chainstitch for easy removal of the hem. Thread the machine with cotton thread in both the needle and chainstitch looper. This thread will hold the hem securely but is easy to remove when necessary.

Serger Lace

Nancy Jewell, Husqvarna Viking

A delicate lace edging for collars or cups can be achieved with rayon thread and a balanced 4-thread stitch. While serging, the right needle rides off the edge and the left needle stitches into the fabric. If working on a circular item, once you reach the starting point, begin your second row with the left needle serging into the previous row of stitches. If you are serging a knit fabric, stretch the fabric as you serge for a fluted-edge finish.

Perfect Flatlocking

A flatlock stitch can be achieved with either a 2- or 3-thread overlock stitch. (The basic nature of a 2-thread stitch formation makes it a true flatlock.) A flatlock stitch can be used for both seaming or decorative purposes and is not difficult to achieve with a little tension adjustment.

● Since the fabric being flatlocked is not being cut, a serger blindhem foot helps feed the fabric evenly, keeping the edges or fold safely to the left of the knife. Let the stitch fall off the edge to the right.

● Stable, tightly woven fabric works best when flatlocking. Trim the edges evenly prior to serging.

● If you are flatlocking a more loosely woven fabric, stabilize the edges in one of the following ways: Apply interfacing to the wrong sides, flatlock over a seam, or fold back the edges of the fabric first before flatlocking.

Flatlocking can be fun as well as decorative, depending on the thread choice you make.

Chapter 4

As we become more and more enamored with

sergers, we are using them for more techniques than

ever before. When determining if a particular serger

foot is right for you, think about what you will use

your serger for. If you do mostly home decorative

*B*est Foot Forward

sewing, you would use a gathering foot or

attachment over and over again. If you make

swimwear and lingerie, you will find the elastic foot

and lace attachments very helpful.

The right foot certainly can make completing a project on your serger easier than ever. Techniques that were once difficult or impossible to do on a serger can be completed in no time with the right foot.

The dressed bear pictured here, completed by the educators at the Brother International Corporation, is a perfect example of using the right foot for the job. Pearls were sewn on with the pearl foot, and the gathers were completed with a gathering foot. The piping was serged with a piping foot.

Blindhem Foot – The blindhem foot has an adjustable guide that allows you to catch a minimal amount of the folded back fabric, so stitches barely show on the right side of your garment. This foot works great on knits and is best suited for sportswear or casual wear.

Bias Binder – This attachment from Elna actually folds a bias strip around the edge of a piece of fabric as it passes through the serger. It's used with the chainstitch formation and folds strips that are 1⅜″ wide into a finished width of ⅜″. It's perfect for creating beautifully bound edges.

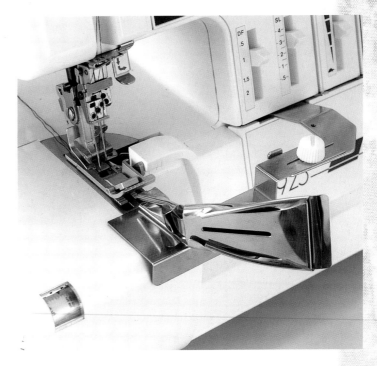

Elasticator – This foot, also known as an elastic applicator or elastic guide foot, holds the elastic in place under the foot while it is serged. A pressure screw is used to adjust the amount of tension (or stretch) on the elastic. This foot may be used with elastic up to about ½″ wide and is used for sewing elastic in active wear, swimwear, and lingerie.

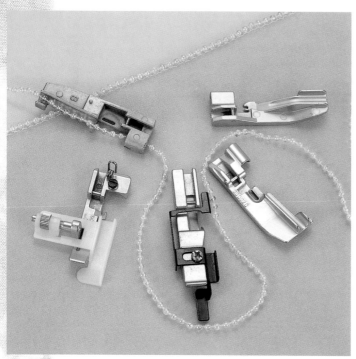

Pearl Foot or Beading Foot – Create decorative pearl edges with this unique foot. A guide in the front of the foot and a groove at the back of the foot allow strings of pearls, beads, and sequins to be fed through the serger and stitched in place. Use on edges, or with a flatlock stitch and monofilament thread, to create an interesting effect all over your fabric.

Gathering Foot – This is a favorite of nearly all sewers. This foot allows you to gather a layer of fabric and sew it to a flat piece of fabric simultaneously. It works best on light- to medium-weight cotton fabrics and is great for sewing gathers on little girls' dresses or creating country curtains. Some companies offer a gathering attachment rather than a foot. The all-purpose foot is used and the gathering attachment rests between the feed dogs and the presser foot.

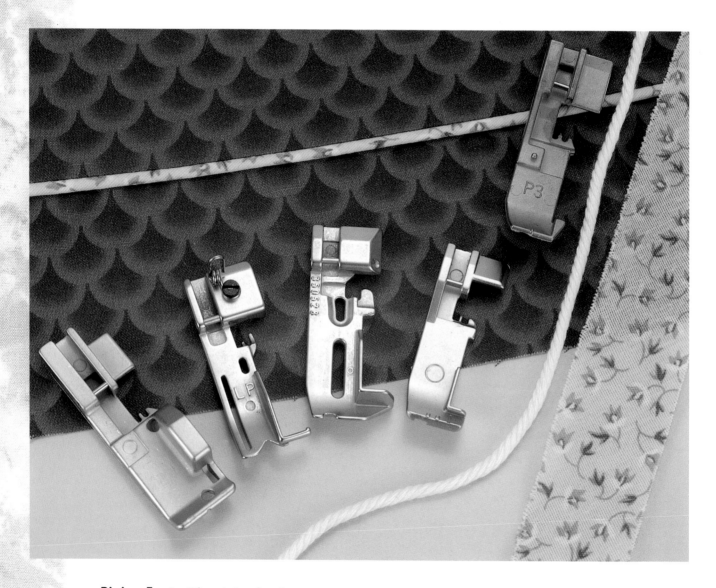

Piping Foot – The piping foot has a groove on the underside that glides easily over piping. Use this foot to serge purchased piping between two layers of fabric, or create your own piping by wrapping a bias strip around a cord.

Belt-Loop Foot – This foot, from Elna, does just what the name suggests: It creates belt loops in one easy step. This foot is used in conjunction with the coverstitch formation. A fabric strip is fed through the guide and is folded and stitched as it passes under the presser foot and through the serger. What a great time-saver!

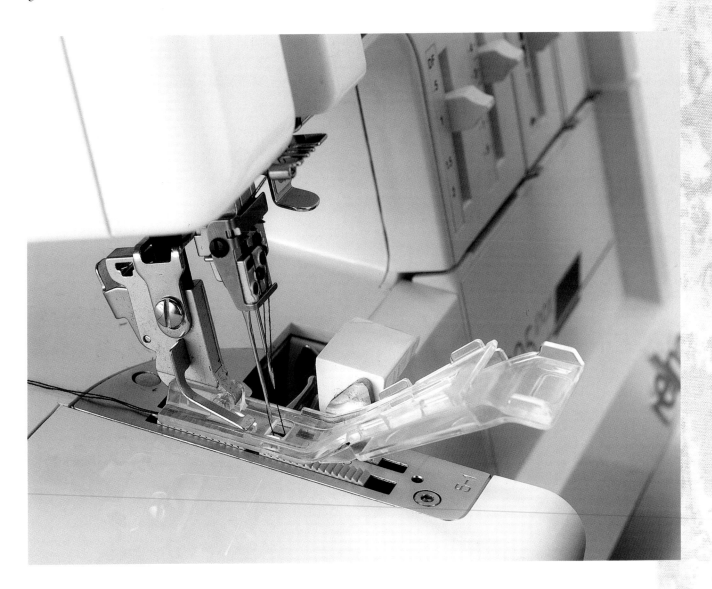

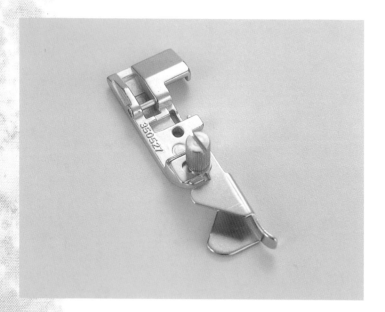

Lace Sewing Foot and Guide – Both of these attachments, one from Pfaff and the other from Elna, are used to sew lace to fabric perfectly in one easy step. The foot from Pfaff has a guide that allows you to precisely place the lace where you would like it serged. Elna's guide, used with the coverstitch hem foot, evenly feeds the lace through as it is stitched to the base fabric with a coverstitch.

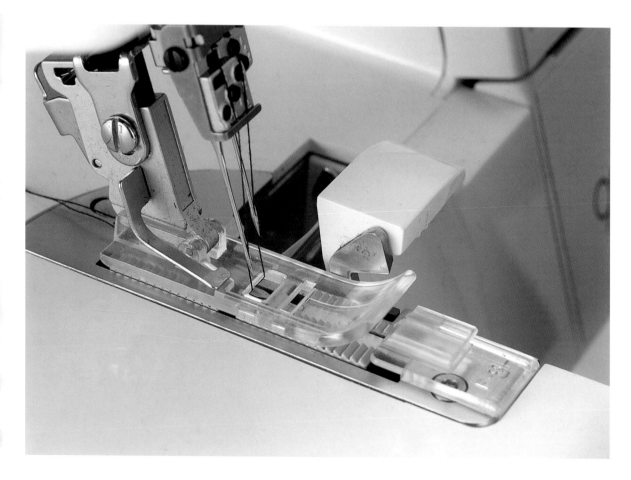

Tape/Ribbon Foot – This Pfaff serger foot is used to accurately guide narrow ribbon or twill tape. It's especially helpful when stabilizing seams in garment construction or for decorative applications such as flatlocking over ribbon. A tape guide may be part of the standard foot on other brand machines.

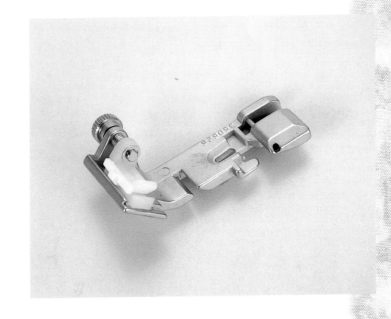

Rolled-Hem Plate with Wide or Narrow Regular Foot – This unique foot and plate combination is offered by Pfaff to allow for different widths of rolled hems.

Following is a listing of optional accessories available from some of the sewing machine companies. There are other sergers available on the market and generic serger feet that may fit any model or brand machine. Be sure to consult a reputable sewing machine dealer when purchasing any foot for your make and model serger. Remember, all of these feet may not work on every model within a brand's serger line.

Bernina or Bernette Sergers

All-Purpose Foot (used for pearls, piping, and
   tape sewing)
Cording Foot
Elasticator
Gathering Attachment
Blindhem Foot

Brother Sergers

Elastic Application Foot
Gathering Foot
Piping Foot
Pearl and Sequins Foot

Elna Sergers

Blindhem Foot
Gathering Foot or Plate
Cover Hem Foot
Guides used with Cover Hem Foot:
   Lace Attachment
   Hem Guide
   Wrapped Seam

Pintuck Foot
Guides used with Pintuck Foot:
   Pintuck Guide
   Cord Guide
Chainstitch Guides:
   Faggoting Guide
   Lacing Guide
   Felling Guide
Topstitch Covered Seam Guide and Foot
Curve Guide Set
Taping Foot
Belt-Loop Foot
Multi-Purpose Foot
Elastic Gatherer
Pearl Foot and Needle Plate
Bias Binder Attachment
Adjustable Bias Binder Foot
Tape Guide
Piping Foot

Husqvarna Viking — Huskylock Sergers

Blindhem Foot 0.5

Blindhem Foot 1.0

Piping Foot 5.5

Piping Foot 3.0

Elastic Foot

Shirring Foot

Gathering Foot

Babylock Sergers

Pearl Foot

Gathering Foot

Piping Foot

Blindhem Foot

Elastic Foot

Pfaff Sergers

Gathering Foot

Elastic Foot

Pearl and Piping Foot

Lace Sewing Foot

Blindhem Foot

Rolled-Hem Foot

Tape and Ribbon Foot

Gimp/Cord Foot

Rolled-Hem Plate with Wide or

Narrow Regular Foot

White Sergers

Blindhem Foot 0.5

Blindhem Foot 1.0

Elastic Foot

Pearl Foot

Piping Foot

Shirring Foot

Gathering Foot

Chapter 5

The serger has long been hailed as an indispensable

machine when constructing garments. This machine

also has become a definite asset in home decorating

sewing. Simple decorative thread changes on the

serger can transform a piece of fabric into a whimsical

Easy Decorating

valance or place mat. Picot edging and faggoting can

add just the right touch and give plain white fabric a

vintage feel. Use the serger to add that extra

dimension to your next home decorating project.

Mock-Mitered Bands

A contrasting mitered band adds a wonderful decorative edge on a curtain. Done with a serger and some decorative thread, this quick-and-easy technique is sure to become a favorite.

1 Cut out curtain panels in decorator and contrasting fabrics. Place the fabrics, wrong sides together, and machine-baste 1½″ from the edge.

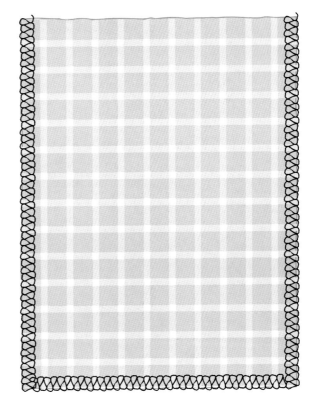

2 Thread the serger with a decorative thread in the upper looper. Serge around the two sides and bottom edge of the curtain with the lining (contrasting) side of the fabric up.

Mock-Mitered Bands
continued

3 Fold rights sides together at the corner, aligning the side and bottom serged edges. Fold the diagonal edge in, aligning all the serged edges.

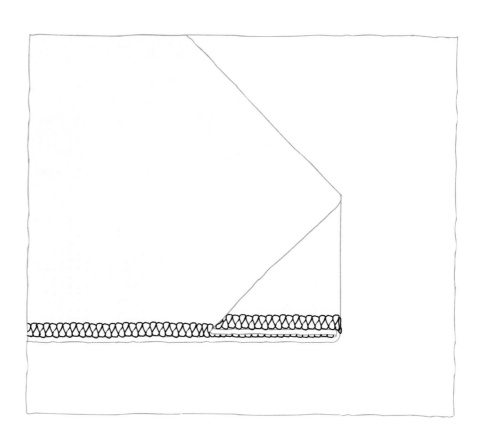

4 Using the diagnonal foldline as a guide, straight-stitch on your sewing machine right next to the fold. Trim to a ¼″ seam allow- ance and press the seam open.

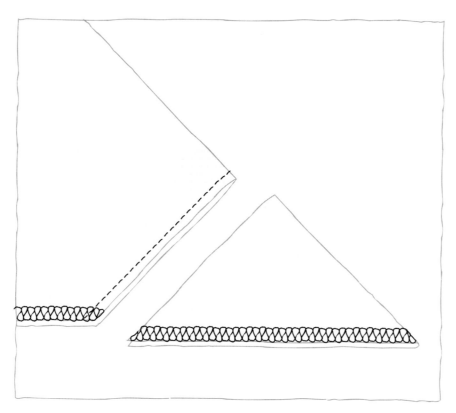

5 Turn the mitered corners right side out and fold the lining (contrasting fabric) to the right side along basting lines; press in place. Topstitch along the edge of the decorative serging and remove the basting.

Double-Edge Ruffles

Double-edge ruffles are perfect for country cafés or Priscilla curtains for your little girl's room. With your serger set to a rolled hem, you can make yards of ruffles in no time.

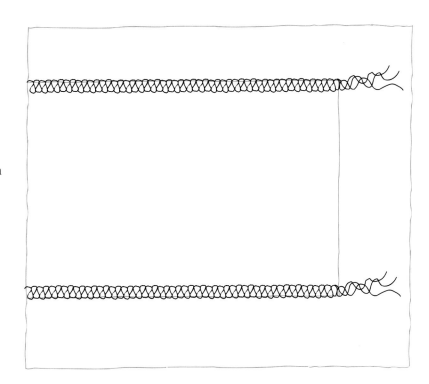

I Cut out a strip of fabric the desired width of the ruffle and two and a half times the required length. Finish both edges of the ruffle with a narrow rolled hem.

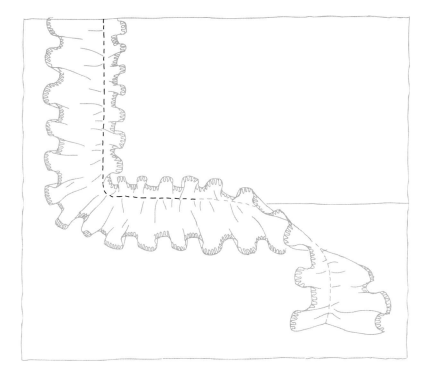

2 Gather the ruffle ¾" from one finished edge using your sewing machine. Pin the ruffle to the café curtain and stitch in place along the gathering line.

Flatlock Hems

Flatlocking can serve both a functional and decorative purpose on home decorating items. For a casual look, try hemming valances or bed skirts with a decorative thread in the upper looper. For more of a country or heirloom look, thread ribbon through the ladder side of the flatlock.

1 Fold the hem to the wrong side of the fabric and press in place. Adjust the serger to a flatlock stitch.

2 For decorative "braid" on the right side of your fabric, thread the upper looper with decorative thread. Fold up the hem a second time to the wrong side. Stitch along the fold of the fabric with the right side of the fabric up. Open out the hem and pull flat.

3 For a ladder effect on the right side of your project, fold the hem a second time back on itself, and stitch along the fold with the right side of the fabric facing up. Unfold and pull flat. The "ladder" side will now show on the right side.

4 Thread ¹⁄₁₆″ ribbon onto a tapestry needle and weave the ribbon in and out of the ladder, skipping every other thread or weaving as desired.

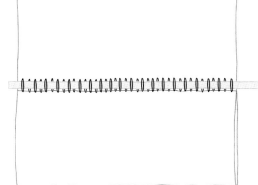

Flatlock Patchwork

The decorative flatlock is the perfect stitch for creating whimsical pillows and place mats or quilts with leftover scraps of fabric. Use fabrics in different textures, such as velvet and satin, to add interest and try a variety of decorative threads and yarns.

1 Cut fabric scraps to desired size squares.
Adjust the serger for a flatlock stitch.
Place two fabric pieces right sides together and
serge a seam. Open out the fabric to flatten the
stitch. Continue adding fabric to create a row of
patches. Make additional rows as required.

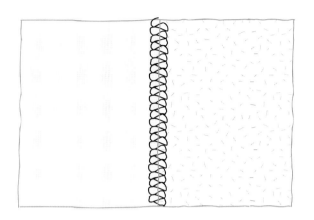

2 Place two rows of patches right sides
together and serge. Open out the fabric
and pull flat. Repeat with the remaining rows.

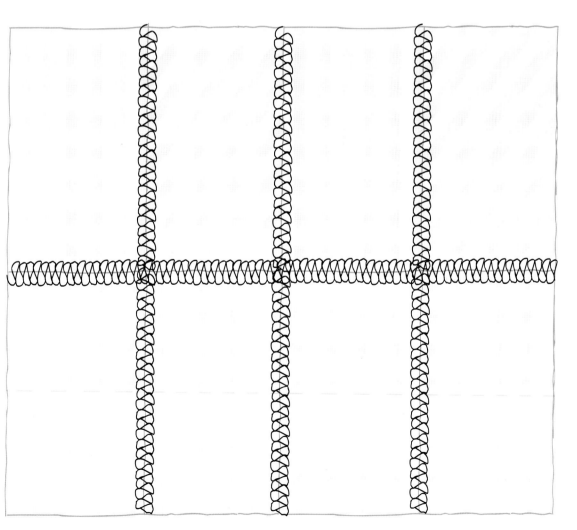

Easy Tiny Tucks

Tiny tucks add a classic touch to bed linens and simple valances. Try adding tucks to bed skirts and pillow shams, as well as sheets and pillowcases.

1 Set the serger for a narrow 3-thread over-lock stitch; for best results, thread the upper looper with Woolly Nylon®. On the fabric, draw several parallel lines with a water- or air-soluble marker to mark the placement of the tucks.

2 Fold the fabric wrong sides together along the marked line; serge along the fold. Continue folding and serging along each marked line. Press the tucks to one side so the Woolly Nylon® side of the tuck is up.

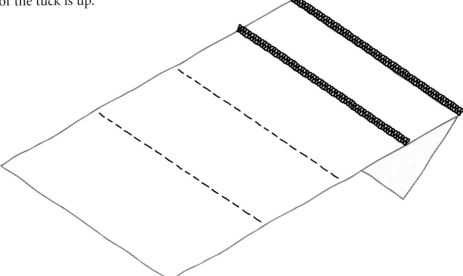

Beautiful Picot Edge

The rolled hem combined with a blindhem stitch from your conventional sewing machine created this beautiful edge finish. Try it on your next set of napkins for a softer look along the edge.

1 Finish the edges of the fabric with a 3-thread rolled hem.

2 Blindstitch the serged edge with the sewing machine. The swing of the zigzag stitch of the blind hem will form a scallop along the rolled edge.

Simple Faggoting

Faggoting is a decorative seaming technique used to join two pieces of fabric. Use this technique to add a contrasting or tonal fabric band to sheets and pillowcases.

3 Place the two fabrics right sides together. Begin serging barely catching the needle in the fold of the fabric, allowing the stitches to hang over the edge. Open out the fabric and flatten the stitch creating the faggoting.

I Serge-finish the edges of the seams and press the seam allowances of both fabrics to the wrong side.

2 Rethread the serger with specialty thread in the needle (it forms the faggoting) and set the serger for a flatlock stitch.

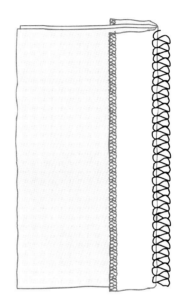

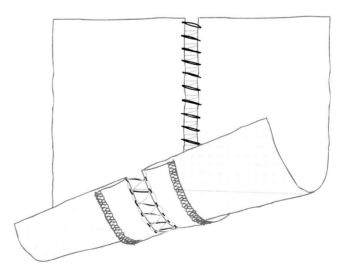

Reversible Wire-Edged Ribbon

Laura Haynie, Pfaff American Sales Corp.

Create beautiful reversible wire-edged ribbon with some floral wire and a rolled hem. Ribbon can be made in any width and fabrication. Try taffeta for elegant holiday ribbons or chintz for a spring tea.

1 Set the machine to a narrow rolled hem with a stitch length of 2.5 and a width of 3. Thread your serger with Candlelight metallic yarn in the upper looper and a Woolly Nylon® thread to match your fabric in the lower looper. The metallic thread should be placed on a horizontal spool holder.

2 Apply paper-backed fusible web to the wrong side of one ribbon fabric. Remove the paper backing and fuse to the wrong side of coordinating ribbon fabric. Cut the fused fabric into strips that are the desired ribbon width.

3 Attach the gimp/cording foot. Raise the presser foot and place the needle in the highest position. Place the fabric under the foot. Thread light-gauge floral wire through the small hole in the front of the foot and place it under the back of the foot, just to the right of the needle. The wire and fabric should extend about one inch beyond the back of the sewing foot before beginning. Sew a rolled hem on one end of the fabric strip. Repeat on the remaining fabric edge.

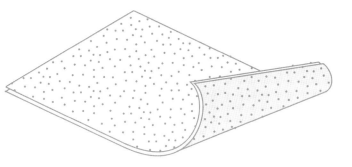

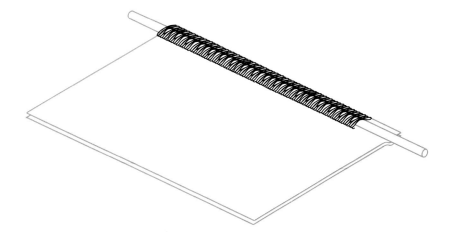

Serger Chain Tassels

Chris Halik, Pfaff American Sales Corp.

Serger chain tassels can be made in any size and are perfect decorative accents for home decorating. Use small tassels on the corners of pillows and for napkin rings. Create larger tassels for use as tiebacks. Experiment with different decorative threads to create a variety of tassel looks. The directions below are for making metallic thread tassels; however, the same technique may be applied using rayon threads.

1 Thread your serger with fine metallic thread in the needle and Candlelight metallic yarn in both loopers. Set the machine for a 3-thread rolled hem with a stitch length of 2.5 and a width of 3.

2 Lower the presser foot and hold the thread tails at the rear of the foot. Begin serging while firmly holding the chain from the back of the serger. Serge several yards of chain depending on your project. The larger the tassel the more chain you will need.

3 Loosely wrap the serged chain around a firm piece of cardboard cut to the length of the finished tassel. The amount of chain wrapped around the cardboard will determine the fullness of the tassel.

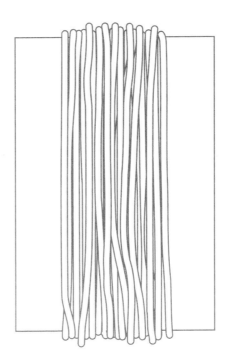

Serger Chain Tassels *continued*

4 Tie a piece of decorative thread or serged chain around one end of the tassel to hold in place. Make a loop from either the chain or decorative thread, and tie the ends together. Thread a darning needle with the loop and insert the needle into the center top of the tassel. Conceal the ends in the tassel.

5 Slide the serged chain off the cardboard and cut the unsecured end. Cut a 12″ piece of decorative thread or chain. Form a loop and wrap it over and around the tassel, ¾″ from the top. Thread the ends through the loop and pull to secure. Use a darning needle to pull all the ends through the tassel.

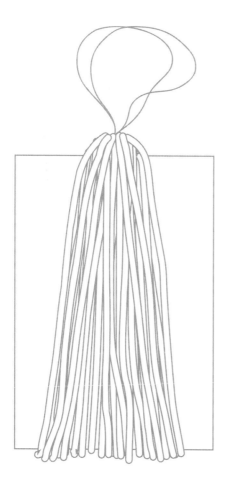

Serger Quilt Piecing

White Sewing Machine Company

Use your serger to quickly and easily sew quilt pieces together. Strip piecing is the ideal technique for creating home accessories such as pillows, place mats, and quilts.

Serger Quilt Piecing *continued*

1 For a place mat, cut two coordinating or contrasting fabrics into strips. Select one strip as the center piece and, with right sides together, serge contrasting strips to each side of the center strip. Press the seams and cut the strip into 2½"-wide pieces, cutting horizontally across the three strips with a rotary cutter.

2 Serge a new long strip of fabric to the tri-color stripped piece. **Note:** It is not necessary to cut the long strip to any length. Place the tri-color stripped pieces, one after another, on the long strip and stitch. Repeat on the other side of the tri-color pieces with another long strip. Cut the pieces apart with a rotary cutter.

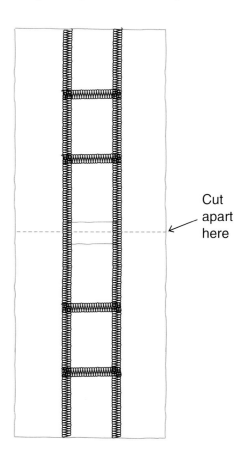

Cut apart here

3 Add a long strip to each side of the newly cut pieces and continue piecing and cutting until you have reached the desired size for your place mat.

Serger Quilt Piecing *continued*

4 Sandwich a piece of batting between the place mat top and the backing fabric. Pin-baste in place. Using a decorative stitch, stitch through all the layers along the seam lines, quilting the fabric.

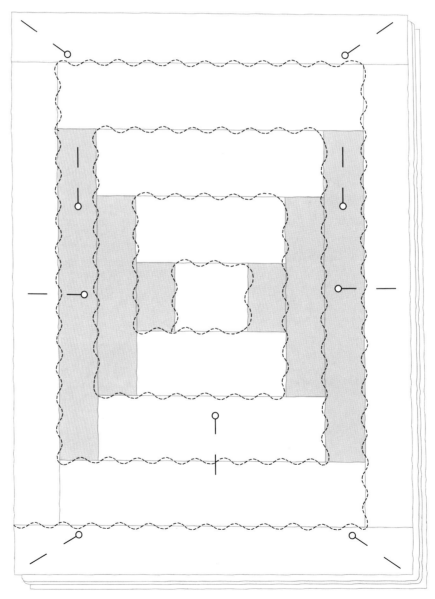

5 To complete your place mat, cut a 1″-wide bias strip of fabric. With right sides together, stitch the bias strip to the back edge of the place mat using your sewing machine. Fold the strip around the raw edge to the front of the place mat. Turn under the remaining edge of the bias strip and stitch in place using a decorative stitch.

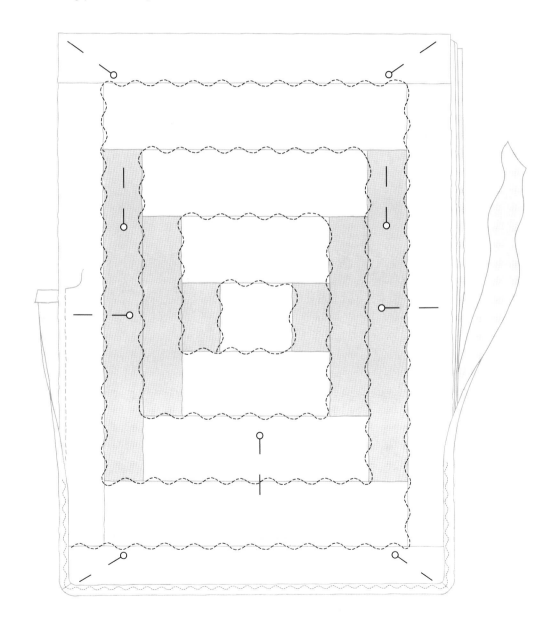

Flatlock Fringe

Nancy Jewell, Husqvarna Viking

Create a beautiful fringed edge on table runners, place mats and napkins. This technique is also great for shawls and scarves.

1 Set your serger for a wide 3-thread flat-lock stitch (needle in the left needle position). Thread the upper looper with a decorative thread, and the needle and lower looper with all-purpose thread.

2 Cut out a table runner, napkins, or place mats to the desired size; be sure to cut on-grain to ensure even fringing. Mark a line or pull a thread 1½" in from the raw edge of each side that will be fringed. Fold the fabric to the wrong side along this line and lightly press.

Flatlock Fringe *continued*

3 Place the fabric under the presser foot, with the fold along the right edge of the needle plate. Serge along the fold without trimming any fabric, allowing your stitches to loop slightly off the edge. Use an optional multipurpose foot to guide your fabric when stitching. This foot has an adjustable flange for guiding your fabric edge, eliminating the possibility of cutting the fabric.

5 Pull the fabric open. Starting at the raw edge, pull out all the threads that are parallel to the serged line to create fringe.

Serpentine Lattice

Paula Spoon, Elna USA

Use this serpentine lattice, made with the belt-loop foot, to create an interesting border on café curtains, tablecloths, and bed linens.

Serpentine Lattice *continued*

1 Set the serger for a coverstitch, and remove the presser foot. Cut bias strips 1 ⅛″ wide by the desired length.

2 Cut a 45° angle on one end of the bias strip. Insert the cut end of the strip into the belt-loop foot. Pull enough fabric through to reach completely under the presser foot. Attach the belt-loop foot to the serger. Turn the handwheel for the first few stitches, then stitch.

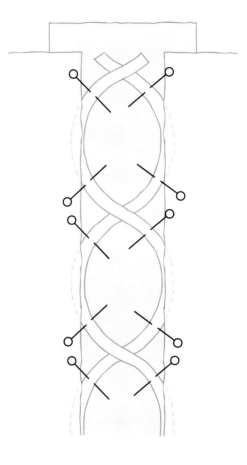

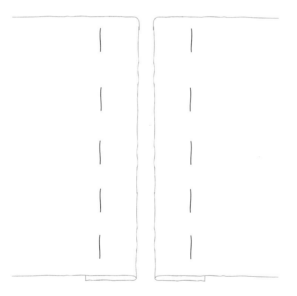

3 Cut your project apart at the point where you would like to insert the serpentine lattice. Press under ½″ on each cut edge. Machine-baste along the fold.

4 Trace an even figure-eight design onto tear-away stabilizer making a template. Pin the bias strips and fabric to the template, shaping to follow the curves. Position the tape so it is barely caught under the folded edges of the fabric at the top and bottom of each curve.

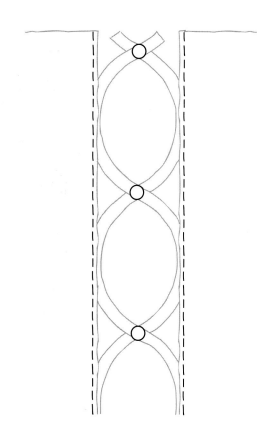

5 Straight-stitch with your sewing machine very close to the folded edge, being sure to catch the bias strip in the stitching. Carefully tear away the stabilizer to reveal the lattice design.

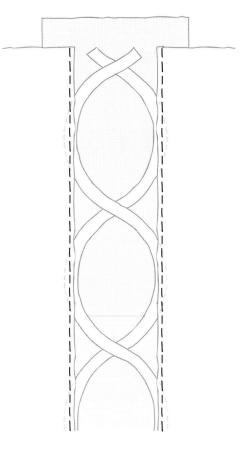

6 Stitch a button or small decorative motif at each intersection to help the design retain its shape.

Serger Insertion

Paula Spoon, Elna USA

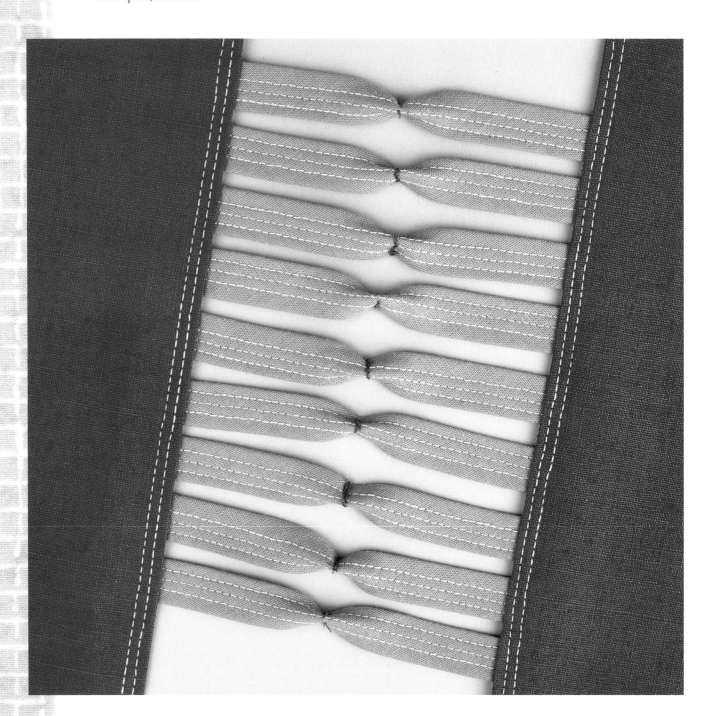

Create a ladder effect with bias strips for an interesting look on garments or home decorating items. It's a great way to add length or change the look of curtains for any room.

1 Set your serger for a coverstitch and thread with all-purpose thread.

2 Cut a bias strip of fabric 1⅛″ wide by the desired length. Cut the bias strips into the required number of equal pieces (the number of pieces will be determined by the width of the area where the insertion will be placed). Cut your project apart at the point where the insertion is desired.

3 With right side up, insert the bias strip into the belt-loop foot. Pull the strip through the foot until the fabric extends under the foot to the needles. Attach the belt-loop foot to the serger.

4 Remove the belt-loop foot and attach the coverhem foot H and the ⅜″ hem/lace attachment guide H-1 to the serger. Insert the long edge of the fabric strip into the top portion of the H-1 guide (the guide will automatically fold the raw edge under ⅜″ while serging). Extend the fabric beyond the back of the foot and lower the presser foot. **Note:** Keep the ⅜″ edge folded under as the fabric is being guided through the attachment guide.

5 Place the end of one bias strip under the portion of the guide holding the fabric edge. Serge a few stitches and stop. Lay the next bias strip under the fabric, again butting one end under the folding guide. **Note:** There is a "wall" under the folding guide that prevents the bias strips from being placed too far under the folded edge of the fabric. Repeat with remaining bias strips.

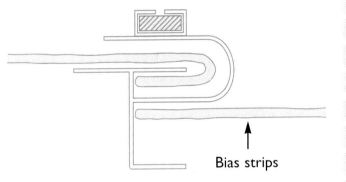

Bias strips

Cross section of guide

Serger Insertion *continued*

6 Create the ladder by inserting the remaining strip of fabric into the top portion of guide H-1. Extend the fabric beyond the back of the foot. Lower the presser foot. Position the fabric with the attached bias strips to the right side of the guide. Butt the remaining side of the strips into the guide and continue serging until all strips are attached.

7 Find the center of each bias strip in the ladder; pinch in half and pin at the center. Sew over each pinned area three times. Clip the threads after sewing.

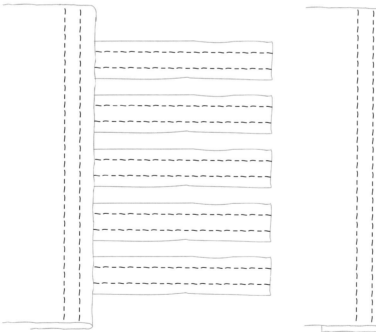

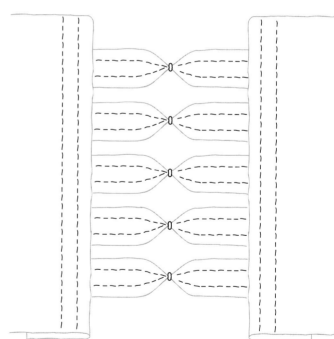

Serger Braid

Kelly Latreille, Baby Lock USA

Create a wide variety of trims by using decorative threads serged over filler cords or yarn. Trims may then be couched in place with a conventional sewing machine using a braiding foot.

I Set the serger for a 3-thread rolled hem with a stitch width of 4.0 and a length of 1.0, and thread the upper and lower loopers with decorative threads. The tensions should be set at 4.0 for the needle, 3.0 for the upper looper, and 5.5 for the lower looper.

2 Feed the cording through the beading foot. The cord should go over the front of the foot and under the guide in the back of the foot. Serge over cord. **Note:** Fusible thread may be used in the lower looper and cord may be fused in place on your garment for placement before couching. When using fusible thread, be sure to use a balanced tension.

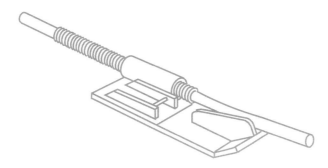

Serger Piping

Kelly Latreille, Baby Lock USA

Attaching ready-made piping into pillows or cushions, is done in one step using the serger and a piping foot.

1 Set the serger for a 4-thread stitch and attach the 5 mm cording foot.

2 Place the fabric right sides together and sandwich the purchased piping between the layers. Piping should extend ½″ beyond the top edge of the fabric.

3 Place the piping under the groove in the foot and place the fabric under the tip of the presser foot. The edge of the fabric should be even with the ⅝″ mark on the faceplate; serge the seam.

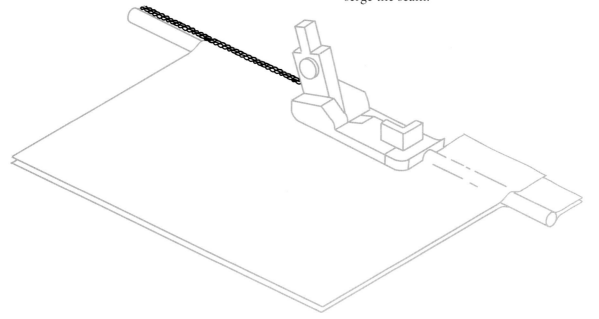

Scalloped Edges
Pat Jennings, Bernina of America

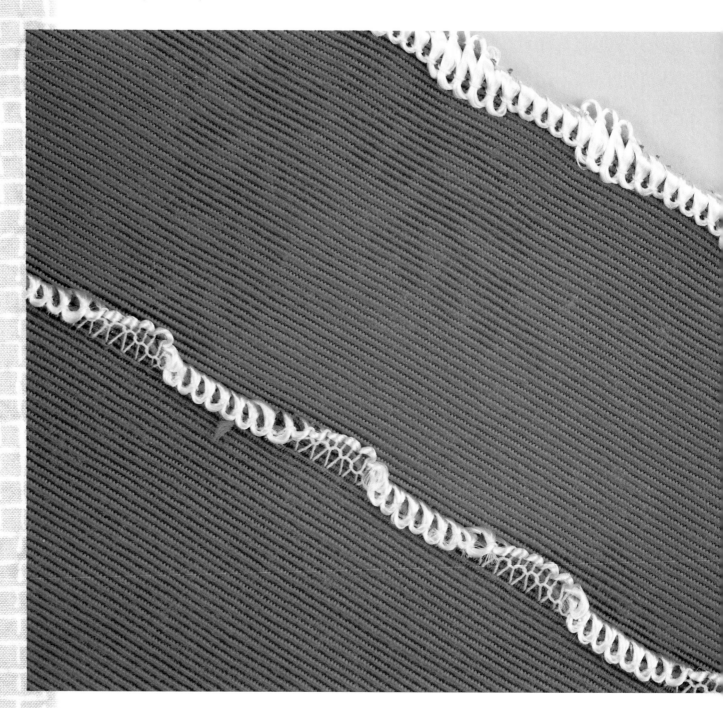

Create a unique scalloped edge finish for tablecloths and napkins by manipulating the rolled hem lever on your serger.

1 Thread your serger with heavy rayon thread in both the upper and lower loopers. Set the tensions for rolled hemming—right needle: 4–5, upper looper: 3–5; and lower looper: 6–9.

2 Serge along the edge while moving the stitch finger lever back and forth, which pulls the stitch in and out. **Note:** While moving the lever back and forth, count to help create equal-size scallops along the edge of your fabric.

Chainstitch Motifs

Deborah May, Bernina of America

Use the chain stitch to embellish home decorating projects with unique designs, such as the mock tassel shown here.

Tips from the Experts

1 Thread your serger for a 2-thread chain-stitch using a decorative thread in the looper and an all-purpose thread in the needle. Loosen the looper thread tension if necessary.

2 Draw the desired shape or design on the wrong side of your fabric. Before you begin stitching, examine your design carefully to determine the best route for sewing. Stitch in the most continuous line possible, filling in as necessary.

3 Stitch along the drawn lines, stopping when necessary with the needle in the fabric to pivot and turn. When all the stitching has been completed, use a hand-sewing needle to pull the thread tails to the wrong side of the fabric. Tie the threads in square knots and secure with a drop of seam sealant.

When changing from one color of yarn to another using the tie-on method, the knot may be too large to pull through the eye of the looper. To reduce bulk, simply cut the yarn and tie each yarn end to a piece of sewing thread. The knots are smaller and will pull right through.
Laura Haynie, Pfaff American Sales Corp.

To remove a 2- or 3-thread overlock stitch, unravel the tail and find the shortest thread—this is the needle thread. Pull the needle thread and all the other threads will fall off.
Laura Haynie, Pfaff American Sales Corp.

The narrow rolled hem often pulls away from the edge of loosely woven fabrics. To help secure the rolled-edge stitch, first sew a straight stitch along the hemline with your conventional sewing machine. Then, when you serge the edge, guide the fabric so the needle stitches just to the left of the straight stitch and the blades trim the fabric edge just to the right of the straight stitch.

Chapter 6

There are many notions available to the homesewer on

the market today — some useful and some not so

handy! Sewing is a hobby full of gadgets all seemingly

designed to make the task easier to accomplish. Each

one of us has our favorites, many of which we could not

The Best Notions

live without. We have listed those notions that we have

found invaluable—those that will certainly make your

serging easier if not more pleasurable.

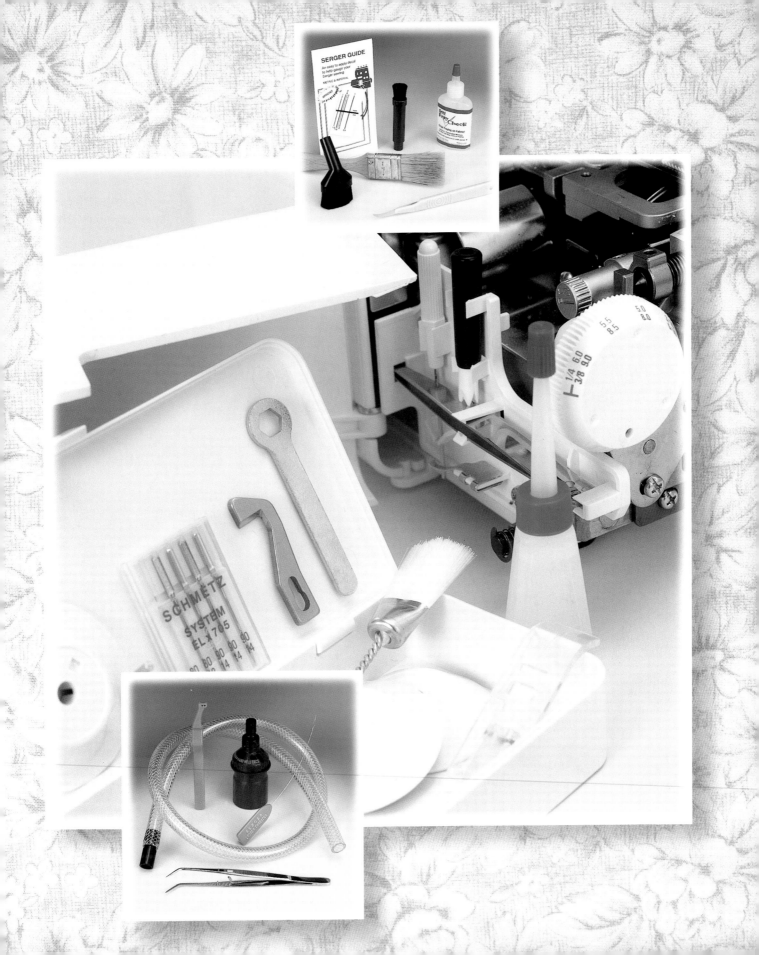

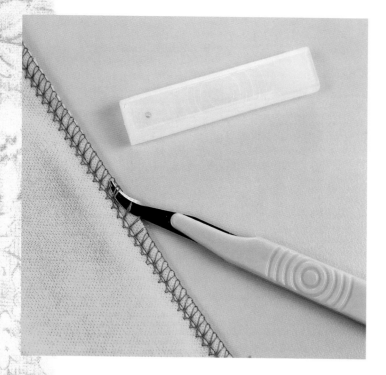

Serger Seam Ripper

As hard as we try for perfection, we sometimes have to rip out or adjust a seam. This task is not usually difficult when sewing a traditional seam, but on a serger, you are now dealing with anywhere from two to five threads in your seam. Removing all those threads becomes time consuming and irritating. The answer to this problem is a serger seam ripper. The sharp, knife-like edge cuts the threads quickly and easily. The protective cover keeps your fingers safe from cuts when the ripper is not in use.

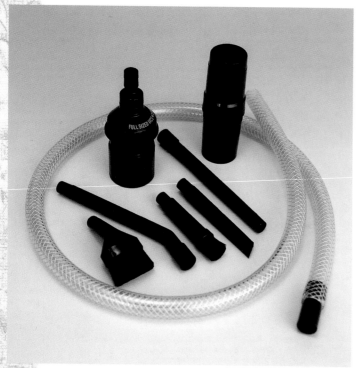

Mini-Vacuum Attachment

Cleaning your serger can become quite a job, particularly when sewing on fleecy fabrics or with loosely wound threads. A handy mini-vacuum attachment sucks up the lint and keeps your sewing area tidy. This useful tool attaches to your own vacuum cleaner and comes with a variety of sized nozzles for those hard-to-reach areas. It works well on your computer, too!

Two-Needle Installer®

Feeling all thumbs when installing needles into your serger? This handy needle tool holds one or two needles at a time and is great for installing or removing the needles. Hold the needle installer in one hand and use the other for loosening or tightening the needle screws.

Horizontal Spool Holder

Have you had difficulty maintaining tension with vertical spools of thread? Do your threads tangle and slide? This horizontal spool pin fits over the serger spindle and holds the thread in position so it feeds smoothly and evenly while you are serging. It's great for Ribbon Floss™ or those threads that are extremely slippery.

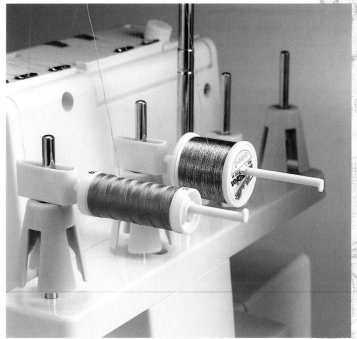

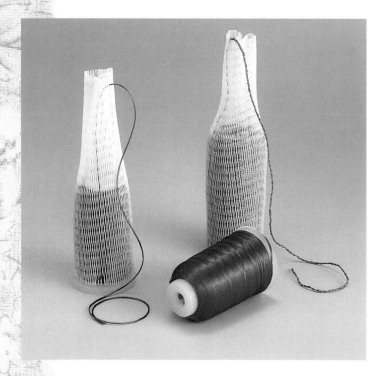

Thread Nets

Thread nets are another handy notion that controls slippery threads. Often included with your serger supplies from the manufacturer, these stretchy plastic nets fit right over the thread cones or spools and hold the thread in place. The thread passes easily through the top while serging. Slipping and tangled threads can be a thing of the past.

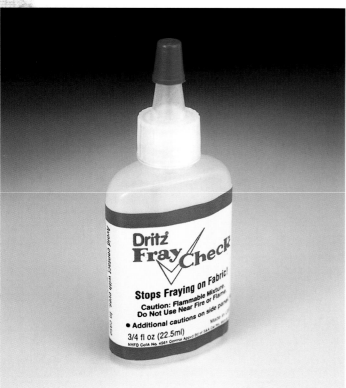

Seam Sealant

Whether you use Fray Check™ or No-Fray™, the results are the same—the threads are sealed and won't unravel. Using a seam sealant is the ideal way to finish the end of a rolled edge or hold threads at the end of a seam. This notion is valuable whether you are sewing or serging. It's also great for runs in stockings, and it's clear, too!

Serger Tweezers

Definitely one of the most valuable tools to use with your serger is a good pair of tweezers. Most every brand of serger comes with tweezers, but there are many more on the market for your use. Be sure to use a pair with narrow points that will grip fine threads easily. Tweezers that lock in place are ideal for slippery or hard-to-hold threads or when you need an "extra hand" for control. Use your tweezers to thread needles or loopers, insert needles, or help thread elastic through the presser foot.

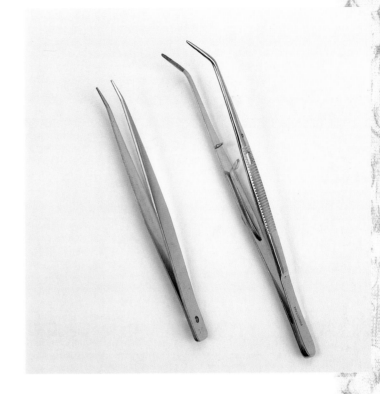

Double-Eyed Needle

This neat tool helps you keep thread tails secure. Use this needle to thread the serger tail back under the previous row of stitches. Now the threads are held in place and won't unravel. Great for threading ribbons or narrow cords through the ladder-side of flatlock stitching.

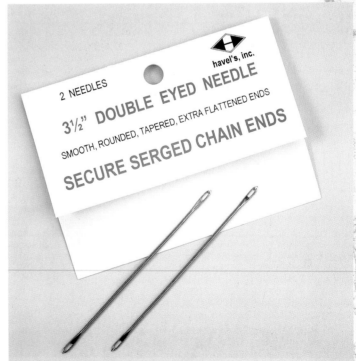

Serger Guide

Having trouble understanding where your stitching line is with the left or right needle? Take the mystery out of seam allowances. This handy decal can be adhered to the front of your machine to help you position your fabric for a traditional $\frac{5}{8}''$ seam with the right needle. Markings range from $\frac{1}{2}''$ to $1''$ for the left needle.

Looper and Needle Threader

The curved shape and fine wire make this looper and needle threader indispensable. Thread any size needle or hard-to-reach looper with this great serger notion.

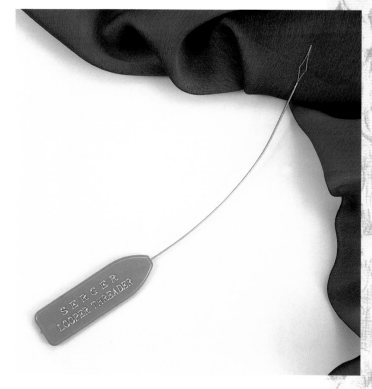

Brushes

Your serger will most likely come with it's own small lint brush. However, having a few extra brushes on hand never hurts. Soft makeup or 1″–1½″ paintbrushes work well to remove stray threads and fabric lint found in hard-to-reach places in your machine. The softer bristle brushes seem to work the best for this job.

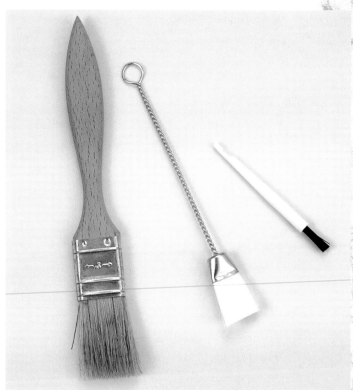

INDEX

INDEX

METRIC EQUIVALENTS

Inches to Millimeters and Centimeters
MM - millimeters   CM - centimeters

Inches	MM	CM	Inches	CM	Inches	CM
1/8	3	0.3	9	22.9	30	76.2
1/4	6	0.6	10	25.4	31	78.7
3/8	10	1.0	11	27.9	32	81.3
1/2	13	1.3	12	30.5	33	83.8
5/8	16	1.6	13	33.0	34	86.4
3/4	19	1.9	14	35.6	35	88.9
7/8	22	2.2	15	38.1	36	91.4
1	25	2.5	16	40.6	37	94.0
1 1/4	32	3.2	17	43.2	38	96.5
1 1/2	38	3.8	18	45.7	39	99.1
1 3/4	44	4.4	19	48.3	40	101.6
2	51	5.1	20	50.8	41	104.1
2 1/2	64	6.4	21	53.3	42	106.7
3	76	7.6	22	55.9	43	109.2
3 1/2	89	8.9	23	58.4	44	111.8
4	102	10.2	24	61.0	45	114.3
4 1/2	114	11.4	25	63.5	46	116.8
5	127	12.7	26	66.0	47	119.4
6	152	15.2	27	68.6	48	121.9
7	178	17.8	28	71.1	49	124.5
8	203	20.3	29	73.7	50	127.0

METRIC CONVERSION CHART

Yards	Inches	Meters	Yards	Inches	Meters
1/8	4.5	0.11	1 1/8	40.5	1.03
1/4	9	0.23	1 1/4	45	1.14
3/8	13.5	0.34	1 3/8	49.5	1.26
1/2	18	0.46	1 1/2	54	1.37
5/8	22.5	0.57	1 5/8	58.5	1.49
3/4	27	0.69	1 3/4	63	1.60
7/8	31.5	0.80	1 7/8	67.5	1.71
1	36	0.91	2	72	1.83